150 FUN Christmas things to DOODLE

An interactive adventure in drawing holiday fun!

Walter Foster Jr.

www.walterfoster.com
6 Orchard Road, Suite 100
Lake Forest, CA 92630

Publisher: Anne Landa
Creative Director: Shelley Baugh
Production Director: Yuhong Guo
Editorial Director: Pauline Molinari
Copy Editors: Janessa Osle, Karen Julian
Production Designer: Debbie Aiken

Printed in China
1 3 5 7 9 10 8 6 4 2

table of contents

introduction to doodling

Welcome to your personal holiday doodle journal! 150 Fun Christmas Things to Doodle is packed with oodles of seasonal doodles. Anything you can imagine—or see with your own eyes—can be doodled!

If you've never doodled before, don't worry; doodling is simple, sometimes silly, and easy to learn. Your imagination, creativity, and drawing pencils can take you anywhere you like. Most of all, you'll learn that fun doodle subjects are all around in our colorful winter wonderland. All you need to do is bring your imagination along for the ride!

basic tools & materials

You can start every doodle with a drawing pencil. Then use markers, colored pencils, or even paint to add color!

drawing pencil
and paper

eraser

sharpener

colored
pencils

felt-tip markers

paintbrushes
and paints

how to use this book

Each section of this book begins with fun ideas and examples to inspire you. You'll find all kinds of step-by-step projects that begin with a few simple lines. Then a variety of prompts will inspire you to take your doodles to the next level by transforming them into exciting scenes!

1

First draw the basic outline, using light lines.

2

Continue to draw in the details.

3

Now darken the lines you will use for shaded areas.

4

Use your favorite art tool to add color!

warming up

Warm up your hand by drawing squiggles
and shapes on a piece of scrap paper.

Draw a square

Draw an oval

Draw a circle

Draw a rectangle

Draw a triangle

If you can draw a few basic shapes, you can draw just about anything!

Circle

Basketball

Rectangle

Book

Triangle

Ice cream cone

Oval

Teapot

Square

Present

Look how you can turn your doodles into drawings!

Butterfly

Tiara

Balloon

Bird

Gown

christmas cheer

doodle here!

Decorate these yummy cookies for Christmas!

15

teddy bear

doodle here!

Doodle some toys under this Christmas tree!

Decorate and doodle these yummy Christmas candies!

20

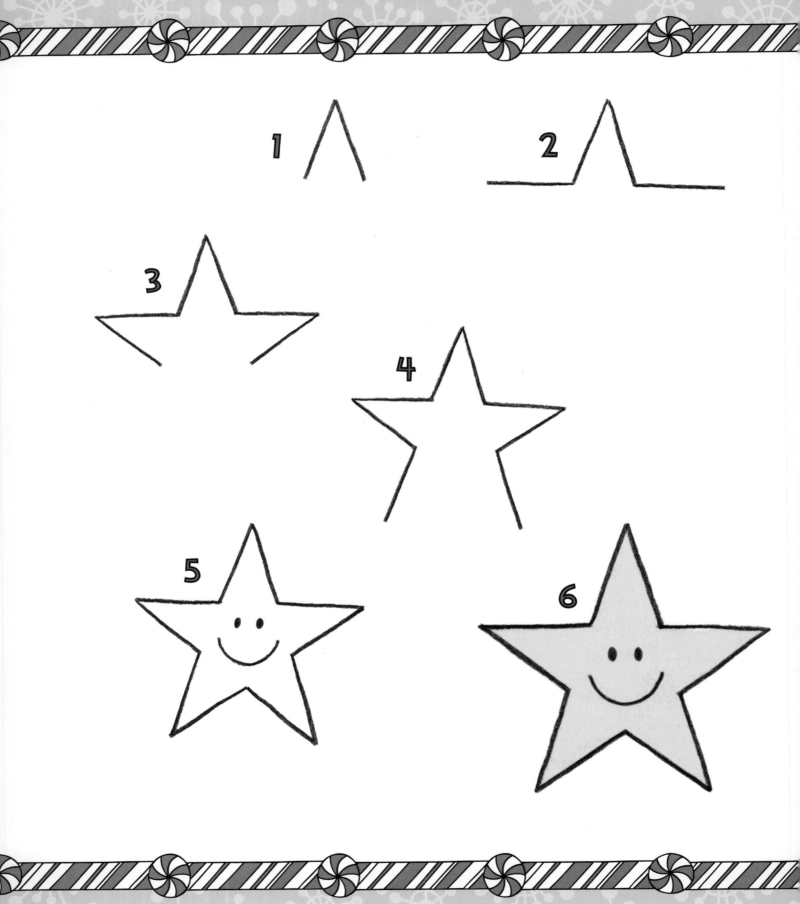

doodle here!

Decorate these Christmas tree ornaments!

Write a gift list
for Santa!

Now doodle what
Santa brought you!

27

1

2

3

4

5

6

doodle here!

What do these kids want for Christmas?

30

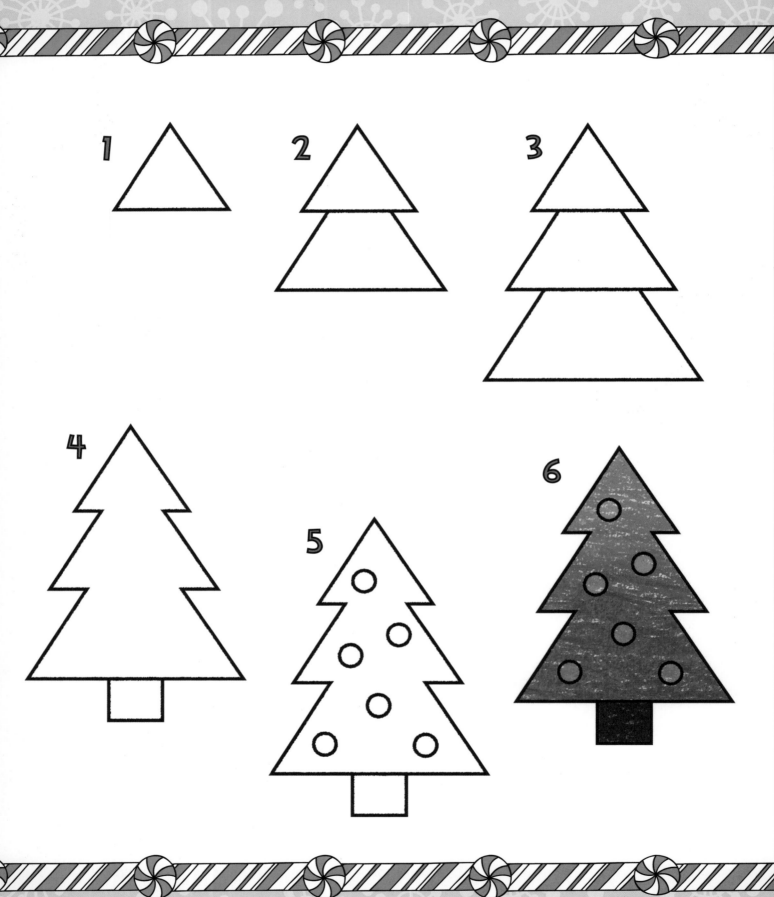

doodle here!

Fill these
stockings with
goodies
from Santa!

Decorate these gifts, and fill out the name tags!

cat

doodle here!

Kittens love Christmas! Give them lots of fun things to play with.

Decorate these Christmas sweaters!

Doodle lights and decorations
on these homes for Christmas!

doodle here!

Decorate this wreath!
Add some flowers and bows.

50

Doodle some pretty gift
wrap on this present.

Draw faces on these carolers, and write a new Christmas tune!

toy horn

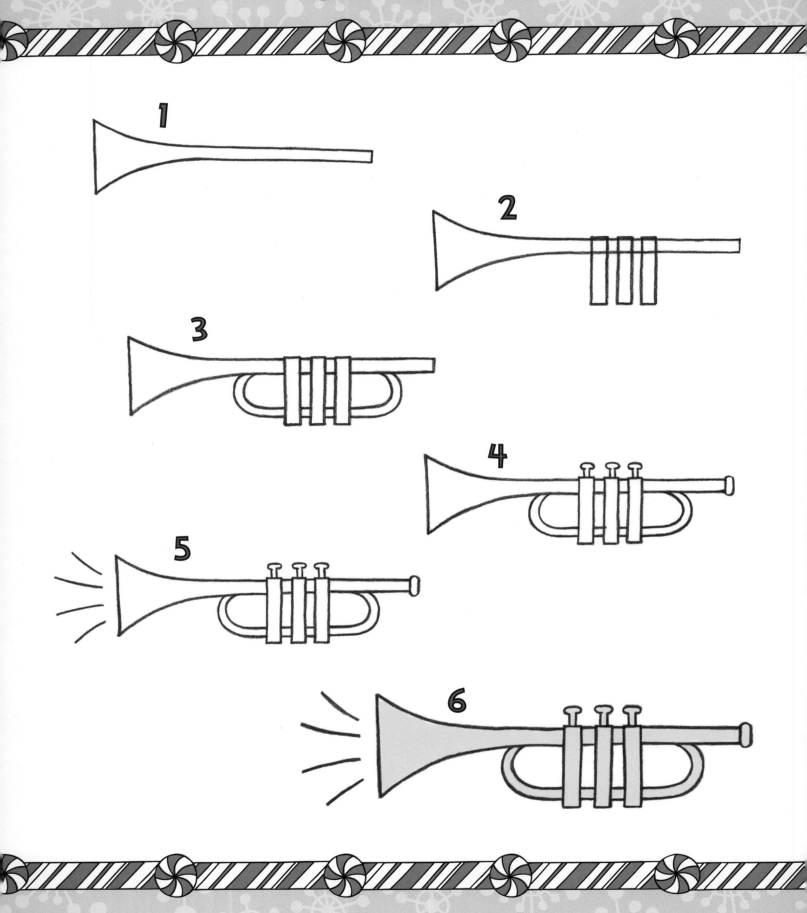

doodle here!

Doodle these stockings with fun patterns and colors.

56

doodle here!

Doodle fun collars
and holiday sweaters
on these doggies!

Help Santa get these reindeer ready for Christmas Eve.

Now fill Santa's sleigh with all of his packages.

Who are you kissing under the mistletoe?

Give this elf
a merry face!

Finish decorating these gingerbread houses. Add colorful candies and sweets!

Color in these Christmas tree lights!

Put on a holiday production, and set the stage!

winter wonderland fun

Help finish these snowmen!

Doodle holiday patterns for these scarves.

polar bear

doodle here!

Doodle this polar bear a friend!

Doodle some colorful patterns on these mittens and gloves.

85

penguin

doodle here!

Add some penguins to this colony.

igloo

Who lives in this igloo?

Fill the sky with snowflakes. Remember, no two are alike!

horse

doodle here!

Where are these horse-drawn sleighs going?

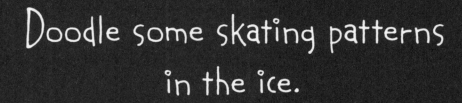

Doodle some skating patterns in the ice.

Doodle some crazy patterns and colors on these winter hats.

doodle here!

Create a winter adventure with skiers and snowboarders.

106

Customize these snowboards and helmets before hitting the slopes!

Doodle these polar bear cubs some sweaters and scarves!

Finish this winter scene.

countdown to christmas

Doodle and journal your way to Christmas day!

december 14th

december 15th

december 16th

december 17th

december 18th

december 19th

december 20th

december 21st

december 22nd

_____

_____

_____

_____

_____

december 23rd

december 24th

_____

_____

_____

_____

december 25th

the end

You've learned to doodle everything from a polar bear and penguins to stockings and Santa's sleigh. That might seem like a lot, but there are even more fun holiday things to doodle everywhere you look! You can find inspiration anywhere—at home or school, in your neighborhood, or from objects right inside your own room. Almost anything can be turned into a fun and silly doodle. This is only the beginning of your holiday doodling adventure!